INSIGHT ⊙ GUIDES

TRAVEL EXPERIENCES
JOURNAL

www.insightguides.com

CREDITS

Editor: Kate Drynan
Author: Carine Tracanelli (Europe), Maciej Zglinicki (North America, South America, Asia, Africa, Australasia)
Images: Shutterstock

DISTRIBUTION

UK, Ireland and Europe
Apa Publications (UK) Ltd
sales@insightguides.com
United States and Canada
Ingram Publisher Services
ips@ingramcontent.com
Australia and New Zealand
Woodslane
info@woodslane.com.au
Southeast Asia
Apa Publications (SN) Pte
singaporeoffice@insightguides.com
Hong Kong, Taiwan and China
Apa Publications (HK) Ltd
hongkongoffice@insightguides.com
Worldwide
Apa Publications (UK) Ltd
sales@insightguides.com

SPECIAL SALES, CONTENT LICENSING AND COPUBLISHING

Insight Guides can be purchased in bulk quantities at discounted prices. We can create special editions, personalised jackets and corporate imprints tailored to your needs.
sales@insightguides.com
www.insightguides.biz

CONTACT US

Every effort has been made to provide accurate information in this publication, but changes are inevitable. The publisher cannot be responsible for any resulting loss, inconvenience or injury. We would appreciate it if readers would call our attention to any errors or outdated information. We also welcome your suggestions; please contact us at: hello@insightguides.com
www.insightguides.com

2018

January

M	T	W	T	F	S	S
1	2	3	4	5	6	7
8	9	10	11	12	13	14
15	16	17	18	19	20	21
22	23	24	25	26	27	28
29	30	31				

February

M	T	W	T	F	S	S
			1	2	3	4
5	6	7	8	9	10	11
12	13	14	15	16	17	18
19	20	21	22	23	24	25
26	27	28				

March

M	T	W	T	F	S	S
			1	2	3	4
5	6	7	8	9	10	11
12	13	14	15	16	17	18
19	20	21	22	23	24	25
26	27	28	29	30	31	

April

M	T	W	T	F	S	S
						1
2	3	4	5	6	7	8
9	10	11	12	13	14	15
16	17	18	19	20	21	22
23	24	25	26	27	28	29
30						

May

M	T	W	T	F	S	S
	1	2	3	4	5	6
7	8	9	10	11	12	13
14	15	16	17	18	19	20
21	22	23	24	25	26	27
28	29	30	31			

June

M	T	W	T	F	S	S
				1	2	3
4	5	6	7	8	9	10
11	12	13	14	15	16	17
18	19	20	21	22	23	24
25	26	27	28	29	30	

July

M	T	W	T	F	S	S
						1
2	3	4	5	6	7	8
9	10	11	12	13	14	15
16	17	18	19	20	21	22
23	24	25	26	27	28	29
30	31					

August

M	T	W	T	F	S	S
		1	2	3	4	5
6	7	8	9	10	11	12
13	14	15	16	17	18	19
20	21	22	23	24	25	26
27	28	29	30	31		

September

M	T	W	T	F	S	S
					1	2
3	4	5	6	7	8	9
10	11	12	13	14	15	16
17	18	19	20	21	22	23
24	25	26	27	28	29	30

October

M	T	W	T	F	S	S
1	2	3	4	5	6	7
8	9	10	11	12	13	14
15	16	17	18	19	20	21
22	23	24	25	26	27	28
29	30	31				

November

M	T	W	T	F	S	S
			1	2	3	4
5	6	7	8	9	10	11
12	13	14	15	16	17	18
19	20	21	22	23	24	25
26	27	28	29	30		

December

M	T	W	T	F	S	S
					1	2
3	4	5	6	7	8	9
10	11	12	13	14	15	16
17	18	19	20	21	22	23
24	25	26	27	28	29	30
31						

2019

January

M	T	W	T	F	S	S
	1	2	3	4	5	6
7	8	9	10	11	12	13
14	15	16	17	18	19	20
21	22	23	24	25	26	27
28	29	30	31			

February

M	T	W	T	F	S	S
				1	2	3
4	5	6	7	8	9	10
11	12	13	14	15	16	17
18	19	20	21	22	23	24
25	26	27	28			

March

M	T	W	T	F	S	S
				1	2	3
4	5	6	7	8	9	10
11	12	13	14	15	16	17
18	19	20	21	22	23	24
25	26	27	28	29	30	31

April

M	T	W	T	F	S	S
1	2	3	4	5	6	7
8	9	10	11	12	13	14
15	16	17	18	19	20	21
22	23	24	25	26	27	28
29	30					

May

M	T	W	T	F	S	S
		1	2	3	4	5
6	7	8	9	10	11	12
13	14	15	16	17	18	19
20	21	22	23	24	25	26
27	28	29	30	31		

June

M	T	W	T	F	S	S
					1	2
3	4	5	6	7	8	9
10	11	12	13	14	15	16
17	18	19	20	21	22	23
24	25	26	27	28	29	30

July

M	T	W	T	F	S	S
1	2	3	4	5	6	7
8	9	10	11	12	13	14
15	16	17	18	19	20	21
22	23	24	25	26	27	28
29	30	31				

August

M	T	W	T	F	S	S
			1	2	3	4
5	6	7	8	9	10	11
12	13	14	15	16	17	18
19	20	21	22	23	24	25
26	27	28	29	30	31	

September

M	T	W	T	F	S	S
						1
2	3	4	5	6	7	8
9	10	11	12	13	14	15
16	17	18	19	20	21	22
23	24	25	26	27	28	29
30						

October

M	T	W	T	F	S	S
	1	2	3	4	5	6
7	8	9	10	11	12	13
14	15	16	17	18	19	20
21	22	23	24	25	26	27
28	29	30	31			

November

M	T	W	T	F	S	S
				1	2	3
4	5	6	7	8	9	10
11	12	13	14	15	16	17
18	19	20	21	22	23	24
25	26	27	28	29	30	

December

M	T	W	T	F	S	S
						1
2	3	4	5	6	7	8
9	10	11	12	13	14	15
16	17	18	19	20	21	22
23	24	25	26	27	28	29
30	31					

PERPETUAL YEAR PLANNER

	JAN	FEB	MAR	APR	MAY	JUN
Mon						
Tue						
Wed						
Thu						
Fri						
Sat						
Sun						
Mon						
Tue						
Wed						
Thu						
Fri						
Sat						
Sun						
Mon						
Tue						
Wed						
Thu						
Fri						
Sat						
Sun						
Mon						
Tue						
Wed						
Thu						
Fri						
Sat						
Sun						

JUL	AUG	SEP	OCT	NOV	DEC	
						Mon
						Tue
						Wed
						Thu
						Fri
						Sat
						Sun
						Mon
						Tue
						Wed
						Thu
						Fri
						Sat
						Sun
						Mon
						Tue
						Wed
						Thu
						Fri
						Sat
						Sun
						Mon
						Tue
						Wed
						Thu
						Fri
						Sat
						Sun

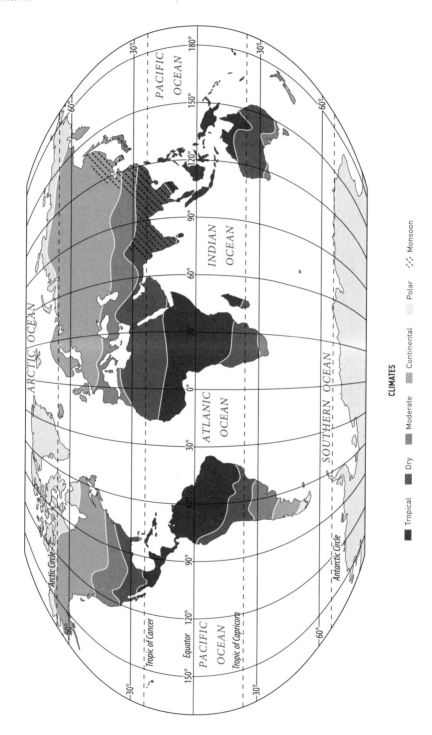

CLIMATES

Tropical | Dry | Moderate | Continental | Polar | Monsoon

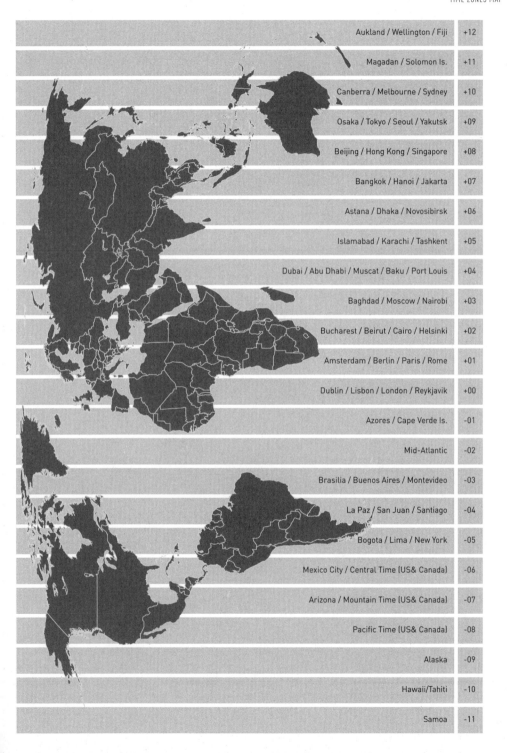

Aukland / Wellington / Fiji — +12

Magadan / Solomon Is. — +11

Canberra / Melbourne / Sydney — +10

Osaka / Tokyo / Seoul / Yakutsk — +09

Beijing / Hong Kong / Singapore — +08

Bangkok / Hanoi / Jakarta — +07

Astana / Dhaka / Novosibirsk — +06

Islamabad / Karachi / Tashkent — +05

Dubai / Abu Dhabi / Muscat / Baku / Port Louis — +04

Baghdad / Moscow / Nairobi — +03

Bucharest / Beirut / Cairo / Helsinki — +02

Amsterdam / Berlin / Paris / Rome — +01

Dublin / Lisbon / London / Reykjavik — +00

Azores / Cape Verde Is. — -01

Mid-Atlantic — -02

Brasilia / Buenos Aires / Montevideo — -03

La Paz / San Juan / Santiago — -04

Bogota / Lima / New York — -05

Mexico City / Central Time (US& Canada) — -06

Arizona / Mountain Time (US& Canada) — -07

Pacific Time (US& Canada) — -08

Alaska — -09

Hawaii/Tahiti — -10

Samoa — -11

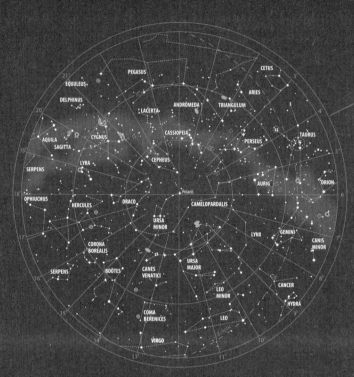

NORTHERN HEMISHPERE

PEGASUS
EQUULEUS
DELPHINUS
LACERTA
ANDROMEDA
TRIANGULUM
CETUS
ARIES
CASSIOPEIA
AQUILA
SAGITTA
CYGNUS
PERSEUS
TAURUS
SERPENS
LYRA
CEPHEUS
AURIG
ORION
OPHIUCHUS
HERCULES
DRACO
CAMELOPARDALIS
Polaris
URSA MINOR
CORONA BOREALIS
SERPENS
BOÖTES
CANES VENATICI
URSA MAJOR
LYNX
GEMINI
CANIS MINOR
CANCER
HYDRA
LEO MINOR
COMA BERENICES
LEO
VIRGO

SOUTHERN HEMISHPERE

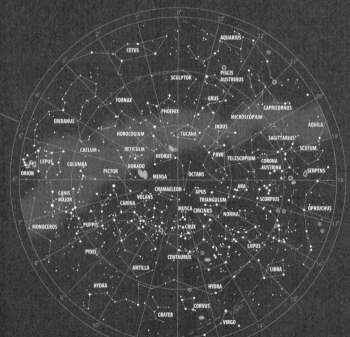

AQUARIUS
CETUS
SCULPTOR
PISCIS AUSTRINUS
GRUS
CAPRICORNUS
FORNAX
PHOENIX
MICROSCOPIUM
INDUS
AQUILA
ERIDANUS
HOROLOGIUM
TUCANA
SAGITTARIUS
SCUTUM
CAELUM
RETICULM
HYDRUS
PAVO
TELESCOPIUM
CORONA AUSTRINA
SERPENS
LEPUS
COLUMBA
DORADO
OCTANS
ARA
OPHIUCHUS
ORION
PICTOR
MENSA
CHAMAELEON
APUS
SCORPIUS
CANIS MAJOR
VOLANS
TRIANGULUM
MUSCA CIRCINUS
NORMA
CARINA
CRUX
LUPUS
MONOCEROS
PUPPIS
LIBRA
PYXIS
CENTAURUS
ANTILLA
HYDRA
HYDRA
CORVUS
CRATER
VIRGO

STAR MAGNITUDE

* under -0.5
* 0.5 – (-0.5)
* 1.5 – 0.5
* 2.5 – 1.5
* 3.5 – 2.5
* 4.5 – 3.5
· above 4.5

Open star cluster
Globular star cluster
Planetary nebula
Diffuse nebula
Galaxy
Milky Way

When you know	Multiply by	To find
ounces	28.3	grams
pounds	0.45	kilograms
inches	2.54	centimeters
feet	0.3	meters
miles	1.61	kilometers
square inches	6.45	sq. centimeters
square feet	0.09	sq. meters
square miles	2.59	sq. kilometers
pints (U.S./Brit)	0.47/0.56	liters
gallons (U.S./Brit)	3.8/4.5	liters
Fahrenheit	5/9, after 32	Centigrade
Centigrade	9/5, then +32	Fahrenheit

Kilometers to Miles Conversions

1 km = 0.62 miles

1 km = 3.1 miles

1 km = 6.2 miles

1 km = 31 miles

Measurement

1 gram = 0.035 oz.

1 kilogram (kg) = 0.035 oz.

1 liter (l) = 1.06 U.S./0.88 Brit. quarts

1 centimeter (cm) = 0.4 inch

1 meter (m) = 3.28 feet

1 kilometer (km) = 0.62 mile

English	Spanish	French	Portuguese	German	Russian	Arabic	Mandarin Chinese
Hello. (informal)	Hola. oh•lah	Salut. sah•luu	Olá. oh•lah	Hallo! hah•loh	Здравствуйте. zdrahst•vooy•tyeh	مرحبا marhaban	你好。 Nǐ hǎo.
Good morning.	Buenos días. bweh•nohs dee•ahs	Bonjour. bong•zhoor	Bom dia. bohn dee•ah	Guten Morgen. goo•tun mor•gun	Доброе утро. doh•bruh•yeh oo•truh	صباح الخير sabaah al-khayr	早安。 Zǎo ān.
Good evening.	Buenas tardes. bweh•nahs tar•dehs	Bonsoir. bong•swahr	Boa noite. boh•ah noy•teh	Guten Abend. goo•tun ah•bunt	Добрый вечер. doh•bryh vyeh•chuhr	مساء الخير masaa' al-khayr	晚上好。 Wǎnshàng hǎo.
Goodbye.	Adiós. ah•dyohs	Au revoir. oh ruh•vwahr	Adeus. ah•deh•oosh	Auf Wiedersehen. owf vee•dur•zane	До свидания. duh svee•dah•nyah	مع السلامة ma' as-salaama	再见。 Zàijiàn.
Thank you.	Gracias. grah•syahs	Merci. merr•see	Obrigado. (male) oh•bree•gah•doh Obrigada. (female) oh•bree•gah•dah	Danke. dan•kuh	Спасибо. spuh•see•buh	شكرا جزيلا shukran	谢谢。 Xièxiè.
Do you speak English?	¿Hablas inglés? ah•blahs een•glehs	Parlez-vous anglais ? par•lay voo ahng•leh	Falas inglês? fah•lahsh een•glehsh	Sprechen Sie Englisch? shprekhun zee eng•leesh	Вы говорите по-английски? vyh guh•vah•ree•tyeh pah ahn•glees•kee	هل تتكلم الإنجليزية؟ hal tatakallam el-ingliziyya	你会说英语吗？ Nǐ huì shuō Yīngyǔ ma?
I don't under-stand.	No entiendo. noh ehn•tyehn•doh	Je ne comprends pas. zhuh nuh kohm•prahn pah	Não compreendo. now kohn•pree•ehn•doh	Ich verstehe nicht. eesh fur•shtay•uh dahs nikht	Я не понимаю. ya nee puh•nee•migh•yoo	لا أفهم lā afham	我听不懂。 Wǒ tīng bù dǒng.
Help!	¡Ayuda! ah•yoo•dah	Au secours ! oh suh•koor	Socorro! soh•koh•roh	Hilfe! heel•fuh	Помогите! puh•mah•gee•tyeh	النجدة! an-najda	救命！ Jiùmìng!
Where?	¿Dónde? dohn•deh	Où ? ooh	Onde? ohn•deh	Wo? voh	Где? gdyeh	أين؟ ayn	在哪里？ Zài nǎlǐ?

TRAVEL CHECKLIST

WHAT TO PACK

Here's a list of essential items to take with you. When it comes to what to wear, you'll need to check the weather for your destination. Check the weight and size restrictions for hold and hand luggage and be sure to leave room for a few souvenirs!

Clothes and shoes
- [ ] Trousers
- [ ] Shorts or skirts
- [ ] T-shirts
- [ ] Shirts
- [ ] Underwear and socks
- [ ] Swimwear
- [ ] Fleece
- [ ] Waterproof jacket
- [ ] Sunhat
- [ ] Sunglasses
- [ ] Walking boots
- [ ] Trainers/walking shoes
- [ ] Sandals

Toiletries
- [ ] Toothbrush and toothpaste
- [ ] Shampoo
- [ ] Soap or shower gel
- [ ] Razor and shaving cream
- [ ] Sanitary protection
- [ ] Contact lenses and solution
- [ ] Moisturiser
- [ ] Travel towel

Health and hygiene
- [ ] Travel first aid kit
- [ ] Painkillers, cold and flu medication
- [ ] Antidiarrheal tablets
- [ ] Rehydration salts
- [ ] Prescription medication
- [ ] Insect repellant
- [ ] Antimalarials
- [ ] Sun screen and lip balm
- [ ] Antiseptic hand-gel and wipes
- [ ] Mosquito net

Gadgets and photography equipment
- [ ] Mobile phone and charger
- [ ] Universal travel plug adapter
- [ ] MP3 player or iPod
- [ ] Camera and lenses
- [ ] Memory cards
- [ ] Spare batteries and charger

Miscellaneous
- [ ] Ear plugs
- [ ] Money belt
- [ ] Binoculars

ESSENTIAL TRAVEL DOCUMENTS
- [ ] Passport
- [ ] Visa(s)
- [ ] e-ticket and flight details
- [ ] Vaccination certificates
- [ ] Local currency and/or US dollars
- [ ] Credit/debit cards
- [ ] Travel notebook

Note that immigration and visitation procedures can change, so always check http://travel.state.gov/content/passports/en/country.html or https://www.gov.uk/foreign-travel-advice for the latest travel advice.

BEFORE YOU GO...

Travel insurance
Wherever you're going, it's advisable to take out a comprehensive travel insurance policy. Check that this will cover the cost of your return flight if you're flown home in an emergency, as well as covering stolen or damaged valuables. Most travel policies exclude certain adventure sports unless an extra premium is paid: take note if you intend to go horse riding, kayaking, mountaineering, diving or windsurfing, for example.

For advice on what your travel insurance policy should cover and what to do in a medical emergency, visit https://www.gov.uk/guidance/foreign-travel-insurance or http://travel.state.gov/content/passports/en/go/health.html

Home security
Set time switches and burglar alarms. Adjust or switch off home heating appliances. Make sure all doors and windows are locked. Ask a neighbour or friend to keep an eye on your property and take in any mail.

For more advice on how to secure your home while on holiday, visit https://www.police.uk/crime-prevention-advice/burglary or http://www.independenttraveler.com/travel-tips/safety-and-health/keep-your-home-safe-on-vacation-9-essential-tips

Pets
Arrange for someone to look after your cat/dog/hamster while you're away.

Further reading
Pick up an Insight Guide for your destination.

EMERGENCY PHONE NUMBERS

Country	Police	Ambulance	Fire	Country	Police	Ambulance	Fire
Afghanistan	119	102	119	Liechtenstein	112	112	112
Argentina	911	107	100	Lithuania	112	112	112
Australia	0000	0000	0000	Luxembourg	112	112	112
Austria	112	112	112	Malaysia	999	999	999
Bangladesh	999	*	*	Maldives	119	102	118
Belgium	112	112	112	Mauritius	999	114	115
Bolivia	110	118	119	Mexico	66	66	66
Brazil	190	192	193	Micronesia	911	911	911
Bulgaria	112	112	112	Mongolia	102	103	101
Cambodia	117	119	118	Morocco	190	190	190
Canada	911	911	911	Namibia	1011	2032276	2032270
Chile	133	131	132	Netherlands	112	112	112
China	110	120	119	New Zealand	111	111	111
Colombia	123	123	123	Nigeria	199	199	199
Costa Rica	911	911	911	Norway	112	112	112
Croatia	112	112	112	Pakistan	15	15	1516
Cuba	106	104	105	Panama	911	911	911
Czech Republic	112	112	112	Paraguay	911	911	911
Denmark	112	112	112	Peru	105	117	116
Dominican Republic	911	911	911	Philippines	117	117	117
Ecuador	101	101	101	Poland	112	112	112
Egypt	122	122180	122123	Portugal	112	112	112
Fiji	911	911	9170	Qatar	999	999	999
Finland	112	112	112	Romania	112	112	112
France	112	112	112	Russia	2	3	1
French Polynesia	17	15	18	Saudi Arabia	999	997	998
Georgia	22	22	22	Seychelles	999	999	999
Germany	112	112	112	Singapore	999	995	995
Greece	112	112	112	Slovakia	112	112	112
Hong Kong	999	999	999	South Africa	10111	10177	10177
Hungary	112	112	112	Spain	112	112	112
India	100	102	101	Sri Lanka	119118	110	110
Indonesia	110	118	113	Sweden	112	112	112
Iran	110	115	125	Switzerland	112	112	112
Iraq	122104	122	122115	Taiwan	110	119	119
Ireland	112	112	112	Thailand	191	1554	199
Israel	100	100101	100102	Tunisia	197	197	197
Italy	112	112	112	Turkey	155	112	155
Jamaica	911	911	911	United Arab Emirates	998999	998999	998999
Japan	110	119	119	United Kingdom	999	999	999
Kenya	999	999	999	United States	911	911	911
Korea, South	112	112119	112119	Uruguay	911	911	911
Kuwait	112	112	112	Venezuela	171	171	171
Lebanon	112	112	112	Vietnam	113	115	114
Libya	193	193	193	* check local numbers			

Country	Code	Country	Code	Country	Code
Afghanistan	+93	Hungary	+36	Netherlands	+31
Argentina	+54	Iceland	+354	Netherlands Antilles	+599
Armenia	+374	India	+91	New Caledonia	+687
Australia	+61	Indonesia	+62	New Zealand	+64
Austria	+43	Iran	+98	Nicaragua	+505
Bangladesh	+880	Iraq	+964	Niger	+227
Belarus	+375	Ireland	+353	Nigeria	+234
Belgium	+32	Israel	+972	Norway	+47
Bolivia	+591	Italy	+39	Oman	+968
Bosnia & Herzegovina	+387	Jamaica	+1-876	Pakistan	+92
Botswana	+267	Japan	+81	Palau	+680
Brazil	+55	Jordan	+962	Panama	+507
Bulgaria	+359	Kenya	+254	Papua New Guinea	+675
Cambodia	+855	Korea (North)	+850	Paraguay	+595
Canada	+1	Korea (South)	+82	Peru	+51
Cape Verde Islands	+238	Kuwait	+965	Philippines	+63
Chile	+56	Laos	+856	Poland	+48
China	+86	Latvia	+371	Portugal	+351
Christmas Island	+61-8 (08 from Australia)	Lebanon	+961	Qatar	+974
Colombia	+57	Liberia	+231	Romania	+40
Costa Rica	+506	Libya	+218	Russia	+7
Côte d'Ivoire	+225	Liechtenstein	+423	Saudi Arabia	+966
Croatia	+385	Lithuania	+370	Serbia	+381
Cuba	+53	Luxembourg	+352	Seychelles Republic	+248
Cyprus	+357	Macao	+853	Singapore	+65
Czech Republic	+420	Macedonia	+389	Slovak Republic	+421
Denmark	+45	Madagascar	+261	Slovenia	+386
Dominican Republic	+1-809 and +1-829	Malaysia	+60	South Africa	+27
Easter Island	+56	Maldives	+960	Spain	+34
Ecuador	+593	Malta	+356	Sri Lanka	+94
Egypt	+20	Marshall Islands	+692	Sweden	+46
Estonia	+372	Martinique	+596	Switzerland	+41
Fiji Islands	+679	Mauritania	+222	Syria	+963
Finland	+358	Mauritius	+230	Taiwan	+886
France	+33	Mexico	+52	Tanzania	+255
French Polynesia	+689	Micronesia	+691	Thailand	+66
Georgia	+995	Moldova	+373	Tunisia	+216
Germany	+49	Monaco	+377	Turkey	+90
Gibraltar	+350	Mongolia	+976	Ukraine	+380
Greece	+30	Montenegro	+382	United Arab Emirates	+971
Greenland	+299	Morocco	+212	United Kingdom	+44
Guatemala	+502	Mozambique	+258	United States of America	+1
Guinea	+224	Myanmar	+95	Venezuela	+58
Haiti	+509	Namibia	+264	Vietnam	+84
Hong Kong	+852	Nepal	+977	Zimbabwe	+263

Days

1	8	15	22	29	36	1	SUNDAY
2	9	16	23	30	37	2	MONDAY
3	10	17	24	31		3	TUESDAY
4	11	18	25	32		4	WEDNESDAY
5	12	19	26	33		5	THURSDAY
6	13	20	27	34		6	FRIDAY
7	14	21	28	35		0	SATURDAY

INSTRUCTIONS

Example:
15 II 1961

1. Identify the year you want in the column "Year" and then find the number in the column related to the month (denoted by Roman numeral) on the same line. → 1961/II → 3

2. Add the number you find to the date you want and this will give you your code. → 3+15=18

3. Find this code's number in the table "Days" and you will learn the day of the week. → 18 → Wednesday

Year / Month

Year							I	II	III	IV	V	VI	VII	VIII	IX	X	XI	XII
1901	1929	1957	1985	2013	2041	2069	2	5	5	1	3	6	1	4	0	2	5	0
1902	1930	1958	1986	2014	2042	2070	3	6	6	2	4	0	2	5	1	3	6	1
1903	1931	1959	1987	2015	2043	2071	4	0	0	3	5	1	3	6	2	4	0	2
1904	1932	1960	1988	2016	2044	2072	5	1	2	5	0	3	5	1	4	6	2	4
1905	1933	1961	1989	2017	2045	2073	0	3	3	6	1	4	6	2	5	0	3	5
1906	1934	1962	1990	2018	2046	2074	1	4	4	0	2	5	0	3	6	1	4	6
1907	1935	1963	1991	2019	2047	2075	2	5	5	1	3	6	1	4	0	2	5	0
1908	1936	1964	1992	2020	2048	2076	3	6	0	3	5	1	3	6	2	4	0	2
1909	1937	1965	1993	2021	2049	2077	5	1	1	4	6	2	4	0	3	5	1	3
1910	1938	1966	1994	2022	2050	2078	6	2	2	5	0	3	5	1	4	6	2	4
1911	1939	1967	1995	2023	2051	2079	0	3	3	6	1	4	6	2	5	0	3	5
1912	1940	1968	1996	2024	2052	2080	1	4	5	1	3	6	1	4	0	2	5	0
1913	1941	1969	1997	2025	2053	2081	3	6	6	2	4	0	2	5	1	3	6	1
1914	1942	1970	1998	2026	2054	2082	4	0	0	3	5	1	3	6	2	4	0	2
1915	1943	1971	1999	2027	2055	2083	5	1	1	4	6	2	4	0	3	5	1	3
1916	1944	1972	2000	2028	2056	2084	6	2	3	6	1	4	6	2	5	0	3	5
1917	1945	1973	2001	2029	2057	2085	1	4	4	0	2	5	0	3	6	1	4	6
1918	1946	1974	2002	2030	2058	2086	2	5	5	1	3	6	1	4	0	2	5	0
1919	1947	1975	2003	2031	2059	2087	3	6	6	2	4	0	2	5	1	3	6	1
1920	1948	1976	2004	2032	2060	2088	4	0	1	4	6	2	4	0	3	5	1	3
1921	1949	1977	2005	2033	2061	2089	6	2	2	5	0	3	5	1	4	6	2	4
1922	1950	1978	2006	2034	2062	2090	0	3	3	6	1	4	6	2	5	0	3	5
1923	1951	1979	2007	2035	2063	2091	1	4	4	0	2	5	0	3	6	1	4	6
1924	1952	1980	2008	2036	2064	2092	2	5	6	2	4	0	2	5	1	3	6	1
1925	1953	1981	2009	2037	2065	2093	4	0	0	3	5	1	3	6	2	4	0	2
1926	1954	1982	2010	2038	2066	2094	5	1	1	4	6	2	4	0	3	5	1	3
1927	1955	1983	2011	2039	2067	2095	6	2	2	5	0	3	5	1	4	6	2	4
1928	1956	1984	2012	2040	2068	2096	0	3	4	0	2	5	0	3	6	1	4	6

Watch the sun rise over the Ghats from the Ganges in India

Meandering through India and Bangladesh, the Ganges River, also known as Ganga, rises in the western Himalayas and flows south to the Bay of Bengal. It is 2,525km long and deemed sacred by the Hindu people who believe that taking a dip helps to atone for past sins and to achieve the state of nirvana (perfect bliss). For a truly mystical experience, take a rowing boat out on to the Ganges in Varanasi at dawn to watch the pilgrims bathing and performing a ritual prayer - the *puja*. It's best to arrange a boat the day before as the price can be considerably higher.

ASIA

SCAN THE CODE TO
ENQUIRE ABOUT TRIPS

SCAN THE CODE TO
ENQUIRE ABOUT TRIPS

Riding the rails on the Trans-Siberian from Moscow to Beijing

Hop on the Trans-Siberian Railway train from Moscow to Beijing, via Mongolia, to experience the unimaginable vastness of Siberia, the amazing Baikal – the world's biggest lake – and the harsh landscape of the Gobi Desert. Covering a distance of more than 7600km, the five-day trip also offers an excellent opportunity to get to know your fellow travellers and taste some Russian traditional delicacies such as *pirozhki* (a cross between a brioche and an ordinary bun) or *cheburieki* (filled half-closed pancakes buns). It's an incredible voyage of a lifetime.

Orangutans, beaches and longhouses in Borneo, Malaysia

Divided among three countries: Malaysia, the Sultanate of Brunei and Indonesia; Borneo is the world's third largest island and a natural marvel. A 140 million year old tropical forest teems with life. Monkeys, including the endangered orangutans, howl in the trees above, while endemic Borneo elephants roam the ancient woodland below. The island is home to the world's largest flower and a labyrinth of deep caves. The Deer Cave is inhabited by three million bats. Deserted beaches are often turtle breeding grounds or, as in the case of Sipadan, one of the world's top diving spots.

ASIA

SCAN THE CODE TO
ENQUIRE ABOUT TRIPS

Road-tripping across the USA, from east to west

Go west, hitting the road from New York to Chicago and then, shadowing the legendary Route66, continue all the way down to California. The 4,500km drive is a quintessential American experience that permits the traveller to discover the beauty and soul of the USA with its endless prairies, majestic Rocky Mountains, breathtaking natural parks, sleek modern cities and friendly people known for their worship of freedom, audaciousness and boundless optimism. Not to be missed is the rich cultural heritage of the country's native inhabitants.

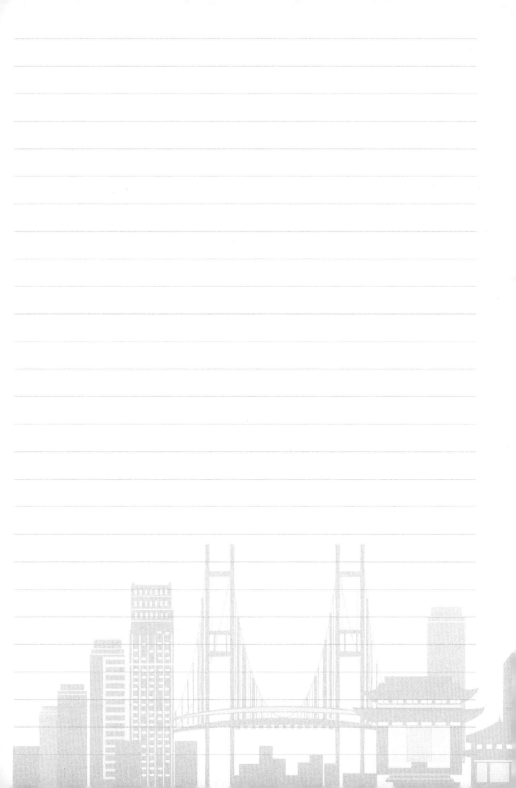

Exploring the ruins of Mayan and Aztec cities in Mexico

From vertigo inducing pyramids to superbly decorated palaces, the ancient Mexican cultures have fascinated Westerners since they first set foot in Mexico in 1517. The Maya and the Aztec used to be the most developed civilisations in North and Central America. Visiting the ruins of their formidable cities are unmissable highlights of any trip to Mexico. Explore elegant Chichén Itzá, Teotihuacán's giant pyramids, Palenque, rising out of the Chiapas rainforest, and Tulum whose ruins perch dangerously on a cliff overlooking the turquoise waters of the Caribbean Sea.

NORTH AMERICA

SCAN THE CODE TO
ENQUIRE ABOUT TRIPS

Cruising around Alaska's coast to see wildlife and glaciers

Discover this remote and breathtakingly beautiful corner of the world on board one of the ships that ply a 33,900 mile (54,500km) route along the Alaskan coast. The views of the snow-covered peaks, tidewater glaciers and abundant wildlife can only be rivalled by the amazing spectacle of the northern lights. Those longing for *terra firma* may prefer one of the shore excursions including salmon fishing, glacial ice treks, dogsledding or bear watching. The most popular cruises last seven days and follow the Inside Passage Route (Vancouver-Skagway) and the Glacier Route.

Exploring the fjords of Norway

The splendid coastal voyage from Bergen to the North Cape and beyond is one of the most beautiful sea journeys in the world. The Hurtigruten coastal steamships make 34 ports of call along this ever-changing coast, some at places no bigger than a handful of houses round a harbour, others at cities such as Trondheim and Tromsø with time ashore to explore. In spring and autumn, the 12-day round trip lets you feast on the dramatic seasonal changes. In May, the fjord valleys are brilliantly in bloom, and the hills and the mountains of the north are still covered in snow.

EUROPE

SCAN THE CODE TO
ENQUIRE ABOUT TRIPS

A journey in Provence

Stretching from the marshy Camargue to the Alpine foothills, Provence is a magical, light-infused slice of the Mediterranean, where black cypresses bend in the breeze under an azure-blue sky, and the scent of pine and lavender hangs in the air. The famous sunlit landscapes and lovely old towns such as Aix-en-Provence and Avignon are matched by the warmth of the people of Provence, who are characteristically full of *joie de vivre*. This corner of southern France is so utterly entrancing that it is no wonder it inspired countless artists such as Van Gogh, Cézanne and Picasso.

Island-hopping in Greece

The Greek Islands rank among the most alluring realms in the Mediterranean, indeed the world. Clean, cobalt-blue seas, myriad beaches, great watersports facilities and up to eight reliably sunny months a year ensure a winning combination. There are some 2,000 islands in total, with fewer than 70 inhabited, ranging from the small, arid islets of the central Aegean, with their whitewashed Cubist houses, to the fertile, forested giants like Crete and Rhodes as well as holiday favourites Corfu and Mýkonos. All are accessible by ferry or excursion boat from Athens' legendary harbour, Piraeus.

EUROPE

SCAN THE CODE TO
ENQUIRE ABOUT TRIPS

Snorkelling in the Great Barrier Reef, Queensland

SCAN THE CODE TO
ENQUIRE ABOUT TRIPS

One of the greatest natural wonders of the world, the Great Barrier Reef in Queensland, Australia is both the largest coral reef on Earth and one of the most accessible. With more than 2,300km (1,430 miles) of mostly pristine coral gardens and rich aquatic life, the Reef supports the most diverse ecosystem known to man. Divers, snorkellers or those who simply gaze through glass-bottomed boats are greatly rewarded. The Reef also has a selection of stunning islands. Many offer off-shore accommodation for overnight stays, from five-star resorts to backpacker hostels and campsites.

Outdoor thrills on New Zealand's North and South Islands

There is no end to the variety of adventure sports in New Zealand. With wide open spaces and a breathtakingly beautiful land full of pristine lakes, snow-capped peaks and unexplored forests it's the place to be outdoors. Whether you like your adrenaline via bungee, surfboard, zorb, or with an ice pick, New Zealand has a variety of outdoor adventures sure to get your blood pumping. New Zealanders have become famous for their willingness to jump off bridges, speed down shallow rivers, or roll down hills inside inflatable balls, and they're happy to help others do the same too.

Hiking the ancient Inca Trail to Machu Picchu in Peru

Nothing can compare with the trek across the rugged landscape of the Peruvian Andes where Quechua women weave rugs and garments, condors soar high above and wild vegetation camouflages the ruins of the ancient Inca cities. As you climb up high mountain passes, feast on the breathtaking views of the terraces, snow-capped summits, wild rivers and some of the deepest canyons in the world. At the end of the journey lies the magical 'lost city' of Machu Picchu – a true jewel of the Inca civilisation. Take a stroll around and witness an unforgettable sunset over the ancient ruins.

Staying in a jungle lodge in the Amazon basin

With the world's greatest river and largest rainforest that contains one tenth of the plant and inspect species on earth, the Amazon basin is one of the world's top tourist destinations. Popular eco-lodges located deep in the rainforest, often accessible only by boat, offer unrivalled opportunities to watch the mighty anacondas, voracious piranhas, colourful toucans and noisy howler monkeys in their natural habitat. Canopy walks, wildlife viewing canoe trips as well as visits to indigenous settlements (some still unspoilt by civilisation) all make for a thrilling adventure.

SOUTH
AMERICA

SCAN THE CODE TO
ENQUIRE ABOUT TRIPS

Hiking across the Perito Moreno glacier in Argentina

The great icefields of the Argentinian Andes spawn a series of glaciers that end in fabulous azure lakes. The most famous of them is Perito Moreno. A 50-meter high wall cracks and growls throughout the day, as enormous chunks of ice fall from its sides, sending waves of water thundering to the shore of Lake Argentino. You can admire the spectacle from a boat but to do it justice hire crampons, ice axes and an experienced guide for the few-hours trek across the glacier. Exploring amazing blue lagoons, bottomless cracks and huge caves is a once-in-a-lifetime experience.

Driving along South Africa's stunning Cape Peninsula

Stretching from Cape Town to the Cape of Good Hope, the Cape Peninsula is a strikingly beautiful region in South Africa with magnificent scenery, lovely towns, deserted beaches and exotic flora and fauna. Driving around the peninsula is a feast for the eyes with wildebeest and mountain zebras grazing on the mountain slopes, cliffs plunging straight into the ocean, penguins colonies at Boulders Beach and the staggering coastal scenery at the Cape of Good Hope. But the highlight is the winding 10km Chapman's Peak Drive, arguably the best drive in the world.

AFRICA

SCAN THE CODE TO
ENQUIRE ABOUT TRIPS

Hot-air ballooning over the Mara plains in Kenya

Every year around June when the dry season starts some 1.5 million wildebeest and 200,000 zebras from Tanzania's Serengeti National Park embark on a 1,200-mile odyssey through woodlands, hills and open plains to the Masai Mara National Reserve in Kenya. The herds are chasing the rain to survive. The great trek is beset with dangers as they encounter lions, leopards, cheetahs and fearsome Grumeti River crocodiles along the way. Observe this astonishing spectacle of life and death from a hot-air balloon for breathtaking views and unrivalled photographic opportunities.